The Little Book to FIND YOUR PURPOSE

When All Aligns for You

Robyn G. Locke

GIVEN BY THE ELDERS

The Little Book to Find Your Purpose:
When All Aligns For You
Published by Golden Page Publishing
Atlanta, GA

Copyright ©2019 Robyn G. Locke. 3rd edition.
All rights reserved.

No part of this book may be reproduced in any form or
by any mechanical means, including information storage
and retrieval systems without permission in writing from
the publisher/author, except by a reviewer who may quote
passages in a review.

All images, logos, quotes, and trademarks included in this
book are subject to use according to trademark and copyright
laws of the United States of America.

ISBN: 978-0-9992458-4-2

BODY, MIND & SPIRIT / Inspiration & Personal Growth

QUANTITY PURCHASES: Schools, companies,
professional groups, clubs, and other organizations may
qualify for special terms when ordering quantities of this title.
Email info@AdvancedEnergetics.org for more details.

All rights reserved by Robyn G. Locke and
Golden Page Publishing.
This book is printed in the United States of America.

Table of Contents

In Appreciation v

Preface vii

How to Receive to Perceive ix

Chapters

1 ... The Synergy of Now 1

2 ... The Flow and How It Does Go 15

3 ... How to Move in Concert with the Flow ... 29

4 ... No Opposition, Only Opportunity 37

5 ... We Seek and Find 45

6 ... Love — the Underlying Key to It All 51

About the Elders 59

About the Author 61

Find Our Books 63

Connect with Us 67

In Appreciation

This incredible journey began in Boulder County, Colorado, where I embarked on employing some newfound knowledge. Thank you, Jacquelyn, for your unwavering support and guidance. Peggy, I am grateful for your friendship and presiding over the many inspirational hikes we traversed along trails in the Colorado Foothills.

A special thanks are given to Lorna, Victoria, Polly, and Andrea for your efforts in making this *Little Book* a reality.

Preface

We seek to provide fundamental knowledge as you begin to consciously co-create your present moment and all the steps that move beyond it.

Surrender to create the possibilities you seek as you move into the expansiveness of what might be as you live from the vantage of possibility and purpose.

Here you will find simple yet profound building blocks to shift the way you perceive and receive insights so you might

The Little Book to Find Your Purpose

move mountains, manifest rapidly and co-exist in the synergy of Now.

How to Receive to Perceive

This book will enable an inner discovery and personal transformation to occur. Might you begin your engagement here when you are ready to be in that contemplative or meditative sort of way? Engage by enlisting one of our many meditations to set the mood. This will enable you to enjoy a frequency adjustment. This adjustment is the best means for a receptivity to occur and for our insights to be more readily perceived and received.

Let us travel this road of discovery together as we embark to provide how each tomorrow might become more effortless. In this way, each new day will seek to reveal more of what you desire to be made tangible and real.

Now you will have the means to enact and bring about all you seek to come into being.

Given by the Elders

Chapter 1

The Synergy of Now

Each day begins anew. This allows for a world filled with new opportunities and their possibilities to be explored. Synergistic qualities exist in all things. Imagine planting a seed into the ground. If you want to grow an apple tree, you would not plant an orange seed in your orchard. What you plant, spend time on, and nurture is what will grow. If an apple seed is planted, it will not bear the fruit of an orange tree. Remember, too, as you move forward each day, you choose how to proceed and what you want to bring into your life. Your choices are as seeds that mature and grow to become fruit-bearing trees, producing like-kind fruit that will be succulent or sour based upon the variety planted. How you feed them will determine their health, vigor, and production.

As you consider your purpose now, do certain things bring you joy and a feeling of expansiveness? Then you will want to do more of the things that align with your positive, uplifted feelings.

The Synergy of Now

As you make choices, you are exercising one of humanity's greatest gifts, which is free will. With this gift, you can choose to follow this or that path, spend time in one way or another, enjoy or not enjoy something. If better feelings come from doing a kindness to another person, rather than experiencing bad feelings when being unkind to another, you probably will choose to do those things that make you feel better. Focus your thoughts on what provides happier feelings.

Understand, too, that free will is a most significant occurrence. Its importance is not fully appreciated, especially when you want to do what's best. Each decision is significant because it sets you on a trajectory which incrementally does change the direction of your life. Even the smallest choice contributes to your life's course. Small decisions lead to bigger ones, and the momentum they create is sometimes hard to stop — although easier to redirect. If you are making choices that resonate with your inner being, you are moving more in the direction sketched out before your Soul came into this body to experience this life.

Choices do impact everything within your life as you reap the rewards or consequences from each decision made. Your life, your outer reality, is a reflection of your inner being. The choices you decide to focus upon today play a big role in how you feel. So what you think, what you bring into your awareness — each plays a role in your world. And it all begins with a simple choice.

It is because of the decisions made that Universe returns back to you what you have called forth. You are a co-creator in this world of form. Do you realize that where you reside today, both physically and mentally, is the result of all decisions that have led you here?

How you align yourself and where you place your focus does, in turn, manifest things similar to the vibration you have set into motion. This will, in effect, return (to you) more of what you seemingly desire. But does your focus reside on wanted or unwanted things? For example, you thought about something you did not want, and now it is here. So simple to bring it into your life, especially when you do not hold any opposition to the thoughts you are thinking. Thus, you can unknowingly manifest.

So you see, although you want one aspect to be in your life, you have drawn forth something that might quite literally be its opposite. It is what you feel, and those feelings do evoke themselves from words spoken. Words spoken, felt, internalized, and forgotten. These are the workings of emotions and their trapped aspects that lie dormant for a time until they manifest in your world. All you have created must be felt and recognized before a release can occur.

Emotions are for humanity, a means to know what path they are on and if they have made decisions in keeping with their desired course of direction. How do your thoughts and their related actions make you feel? You may have heard it said — *If it doesn't feel good, choose a different thought.* Choose to think and do those things that make you feel good and generally more at peace with life.

From this vantage, know you are meant to experience life with all of its trappings, not just certain things. This is the actual reason you have incarnated into this physical form. You have come here to experience life and to fully feel all of your creations. Not to think you know how something feels as if you were reading a textbook, but to actually feel the emotions created by embracing each experience.

Do you believe much of the world revolves around you, and even in another's story, you are somehow in the midst of what is being shared? Do you try to find the similarity or correlation? Are they telling you this story to make some point about you?

You use your life experience filters to define a story a friend shares and any special meaning behind their story. By the time their storytelling is finished, you have created some drama on various points, but you do not stop to clarify these nuances. You allow for the continuation of the story, and soon the conversation has changed focus. As in most social settings, you move onto another topic.

Shortly you lose recall of the specific points within the story that may have ruffled your feathers. Yet the body remembers you had some angst on various points. So not able to fully feel the effects of the words that were spoken, these sound-bites and the emotions they stirred in you when left unexpressed became stored, tucked down, and layered upon.

In time, this trapped energy will gather more of its kind, resurfacing as an ache, pain, or some other discomfort. *Gee, I wasn't doing anything to have caused this pain ... why is this happening to me? What did I do to cause this?* These things were caused by former, unexpressed thoughts, emotions, and the feelings they equated to when internalized. Acknowledge and feel each thing to enable a quick release to occur.

Once felt, each energetic creation can melt away and dissipate. Otherwise, this energy, known as emotions, may remain trapped. They do energetically shift all within their proximity as these unexpressed emotions become stored. Later this latent energy appears in your body as a discomfort, ache, pain, or disease.

Do recognize that pain can be a blessing if you see the benefit it offers. Yes, that may sound strange, but what other indicator do you have in a world where so much of life is trapped within the mind? The mind and its trappings create a web of intrigue with its stories and dramas.

Ego will routinely take the opposite viewpoint to keep you as its host engaged, regardless of the position taken. Yes, the old fight or flight aspect of ego is launched. Truly it does not matter if the host lives or dies as long as ego has maintained the relevance of its rantings. Its ongoing purpose has now been newly satisfied. In this way, it can continue in the ravages it creates. It's not personal — it is as it is. So much so that life can be a torment and painful experience, as opposed to experiencing the joy and creative expanse intended for each Soul embodied here.

It is rather foolhardy to expect something so primal as ego to understand life from a more elevated stature. Thus, ego can take either side of an argument and never lacks an opinion or words. Ego's original purpose was to protect its host (you) while anticipating any occurrence that might endanger it.

Ego can be your worst companion or

best friend. Best friend when you have something from which you need protection and worst companion most other times. So, being aware of the mental trappings that go on upstairs is most important as you become the monitor of the endless mental chatter that goes on there. In observing and not judging, see the folly of what is being bantered about.

It's quite entertaining when you look at ego in this way and do not give stock or weight to its many judgments. What does it matter how someone looks, or if their hair is just so? Is their talk meant to infringe on your rights, or are they only making small talk? The drama and storyline created in the mind are just that — a drama, a story. You do not even know if any of these assumptions are true. In most cases, they are not. They do create dramas that play on in the mind, though. The rambling dialog continues and seemingly never stops. This is where you become the guardian of what flows between your two ears. Monitor your thoughts. Are they uplifting or judgmental in nature? Know you are not to be the judge and jury for every occurrence that flashes before you. Surely your mission and role in this life is something of greater value than being the judge and jury for each activity you encounter. To what purpose and to whose benefit does placing judgment serve anyway?

Once you are more fully aware of such folly, you can become the Awareness and engage in the day in a more conscious way.

It is this that leads you to know of the flow and how it does go.

Chapter 2

The Flow and How It Does Go

As you look at your current path, when you shift your focus and thoughts, you will change your attitude and demeanor. Do this first to move out of recurring negative ideas that might keep you trapped in a mental loop. This will allow you to see new choices with differing outcomes. So how do you enter the flow of Universal consciousness, and what will keep you there?

You will need to get out of the way of your own limitations to engage in this mighty river of life. Remove the mental blocks to what is going on around you in order to sustain and remain there — as you bring forward all you desire to manifest within this life.

Do you have a long-held dream or ambition that is waiting to be born? Can you bring it into your awareness now and allow it to be prominent in some way? Dreams are those things that make your heart sing and bring joy to your being. This is why you have come here ... to create, manifest, and share unique experiences.

So how is it (by entering into this flow) that you can also allow what is to be? It is by shifting out of your head and into your

The Flow and How It Does Go

heart. It is to discover your heart's desire as it awaits manifestation. This thing you are to bring forward is your unique quality or gift. Only you have the ability and vision to bring it forth in your unique manner. It is what makes work play and becomes an extension of you as it resonates so deeply within. This gift yearns to break free from a self-made prison of limitation and lack. This is where it has been confined and restricted entrance into this world of form. In time, you are meant to experience your true expression, your purpose, and to manifest it into this reality. Discover what is awaiting its entrance into this world. It waits for your focused attention and the desire to physically bring it into being.

Enter into the energetic space where there is no start or finish. It is as it was yesterday and continues to be today. In the flow of consciousness, you do access a warehouse of measure that energetically holds all you might bring forth into this life so that you might experience ultimate happiness or mirth. Mirth in that happiness is sometimes fleeting, yet mirth is what resonates from a higher vibrational frequency. It allows a deep-seated contentedness to come forward and express itself into this world of form. A very similar yet different vibration to it is joy.

Enter into the flow of consciousness. You reside in the flow of Universal consciousness as you do those things that resonate with you and your Essence. But

The Flow and How It Does Go

how do you get there? It is when you stay in a positive state of being. You will feel it in your heart and experience it through your actions, which we often refer to as *doings*. Know what you seek is attainable when you stay out of the negative *what ifs* mentally projected upon you. You can always listen to the banter of the mind and allow it to draw you down. Choose rather to shift into a *what is* thought instead. These thoughts will propel you into the flow of consciousness. It is really that easy. So when you have the option to think an uplifting thought or one that makes you feel sad or brings you less fulfillment, less joy, less laughter, choose the happier choice. Choose to think upon happier concepts, as you are the gatekeeper of all of your thoughts and feelings. Shut the door to those negative *what ifs* to allow other possibilities to enter in. Thoughts create feelings, and feelings create emotions. Emotions bring forth actions or reactions, and these result in your manifested reality.

Remember, though, it all begins with a single thought. Choose those things that bring a smile to your face and allow joy to enter your heart. Then you are on the path to getting into the flow. Once there, you will never want to leave this state of contentedness. It will draw you into other similar thoughts. Each will propel you a bit higher in vibrational bliss. One upon the other will build and draw you into something akin to a whirlwind. You are enveloped by a momentum that is limitless and

The Flow and How It Does Go

unbounded. Know too, all is possible when operating from a state of surrender when you do not predetermine each outcome.

How can other possibilities reveal themselves to you when you have operated from a place of already knowing each thing? You have already determined how they will turn out. Can you really know with certainty any outcome? It is when you enter into a state of not knowing, a state of wonder, that other possibilities can then enter in too.

Contemplate and recognize you cannot know all. Seek for the unknown to become known to you through surrender. It is from this state of allowing that more can readily enter in. Allow for other outcomes to come into play. When all is already known, how can life's mystery enter in to surprise you?

So here is something you can do that has not yet been practiced but by a few. Sit with the intention to draw higher frequencies to you. What do we mean by this? Center yourself and recognize that all life, as is your being, is composed of atoms. Atoms can change their spin, their rotation when their frequency changes. When they are recalibrated in this manner, they can out-picture a different pattern than they held before.

So how do you change your frequency and what can be done to elevate things in such a way that can also shift the rotational spin of an atom? It is the vibrational frequency that allows for this change to occur. By making slight modifications, these higher frequencies can be a part of your daily moment-to-moment life. Drawing forth higher frequencies is something that has been a part of mankind's earlier history yet has been lost for a time. So in reintroducing it, we seek your undivided attention and ask that you enter into this teaching when you are ready to access a more elevated state.

To elevate your frequency, let's do a little tune-up. Begin when you have quiet time to devote to this topic. In that way, you can experience the full measure of what is being conveyed … as it is distinct and unique to our discussion now.

Hold this in your mind's eye as you shift your focus to elevate your personal frequency. In doing so, you will simultaneously raise your consciousness. This shift

The Little Book to Find Your Purpose

will create a buoyancy that can be engaged even when you feel downtrodden.

Sit in a comfortable position and focus on the following lines. It is this mantra and the subsequent verses that will provide you with a geometric rhythm which will resonate within your being. In its repetition, your consciousness can be elevated and raised to a level that will allow you to outwit the mind in its unending banter.

These words will shut down its chatter by slowing the ramblings there. In this way, you can create a peace beyond human understanding as this creates an ebb and flow within you like no other. Focus, remain centered, and now begin —

Mantra and Verse

Om Bava Shanti (3x)
Shanti Allah Hum.

Om Bava Shanti (3x)
    Shanti Allah Hum.

~~~

Always present, yet now so bright
the Flame within me does now ignite.

It is burning through my body this day,
    and does race like a bonfire to clear away
    all in discord, not aligned within,
    does consume and expand as we begin.

Mantra and Verse
(continued)

Do know that Light and Love
do fill all vacuums and voids.

They do illuminate and grow,
    eliminate what's buried below.

We now seek to remove that which hinders
    your life force,
    to go and do and Be, of course.

So move this day, empowered, and know
    that this breaks up, consumes what blocks
    your flow.

Now you are in the momentum of Love
    as this resonates and restores your Essence
    from below to above.

For you are more than a mere body, you see,
    and as such, do command to now be set free.

The Flow and How It Does Go

It is in the repetition of these lines that a synergistic energy is created, and a raising or buoying of energy occurs. In this simple act of surrender to the words and their essence, much can be shifted and re-engineered.

The components that have been given to restructure a life in need of assistance are miraculous. So many aspects within life are miracles in motion. Beginning with the movement of the sun and stars to the birth of a child, from creation and existence to seasonal cycles, all are miraculous in their core essence. Life is amazing. And to *not* recognize this and to *not* stay in a state of awe throughout the day is *not* entering into its sacredness. If you were to walk around and focus on the marvels that exist in nature, you would truly allow your body a reset of sorts. A chance to breathe and be present, rather than rushing through life as you race to the next activity. So pause as you stay conscious of your surroundings to more easily enter and thus tarry longer in Universal flow.

Chapter 3

How to Move in Concert with the Flow

The flow mentioned in the last chapter will bring you to that space where you will recognize choices that allow you to remain in the flow or know when you have moved outside of it. This moves us to the next facet of being, which is consciousness in flow.

It is always your choice to engage life at one level or another. It is not to say that one is higher or better, but when objectives can come to you at a faster, almost breakneck speed, wouldn't you prefer to be caught up in that energetic whirlwind? Wouldn't you prefer to undertake objectives that move you toward your purpose, sooner rather than later, and to do so in a healthy body while enjoying a happier state of mind?

We seek your wholeness, good health, and happiness. Thus, we provide a road map, so to speak, to guide you to a more expedient path leading to the destination you desire. A path will lead you to a road, which turns into a highway. All will get you to your destination, but the speed at which you travel and arrive is the difference you will experience. Why take the longer route when a highway of travel will get you where you desire to be so much faster?

So, being in the flow, as we have said, is a welcome space in which to be. Momentum is already a part of the flow that moves you, and so rather than you working, set Universe to work on fulfilling your objectives. You carve out what you want, outlining or perhaps detailing certain points for Universe to know. Universe then sets out to deliver more of your focused attention back to you. Will you be amazed when all, plus other unimagined aspects, are provided?

Begin by maintaining positive thoughts. When you engage in uplifted thoughts, those that make you happy, you will enter into the flow garnering momentum as you add purpose to the equation. This will transport a slow-moving scenario into one of high speed and staggeringly quick outcomes. These positive thoughts will keep you in this energetic whirlwind, some know as the vortex. It is a spectacular place to be, and we seek your alignment with Universe by employing this first activity: positive thought. This will allow you to go into this most preferred energetic space, maintain your ability to stay there longer while doing so with great ease.

Remain in the flow of consciousness. It need not be difficult. You do not need to be of a certain age to enter. Our desire is to relate this knowledge to those of any age who are young at heart. Forming early habits before the mind must be retrained

How to Move in Concert with the Flow

would be the easiest. When you implement and strive to stay engaged in positive thinking throughout the day, the fruits produced will yield unexpected outcomes that will buoy up everything that follows such thinking. You are the creator of all things within your life. Thus, this will allow for unprecedented advancements to be experienced and for you to more readily enjoy the fruits of your creation. This is most critical to understand.

When you engage and practice this teaching, new opportunities can come to you at any age. Age is only a number and a state of mind. Know that if you choose, you can become ageless in these endeavors. Do not limit what you want to accomplish by a perceived number that has no real value, except to remind you that you have time yet to continue and achieve.

It is really about keeping track of what runs in your mind's eye and refocusing on better, more positive thoughts — if that is the current need. Redirect to positive ideas, ones that make you feel good. Perhaps the term happier thoughts is a better way to describe this. Engage with those things that produce good emotions and good feelings within you — especially as you are the best one to know if something resonates positively and appropriately within. Keep track of this and know that as soon as an idea shifts outside of what brings a smile to your face, then it is time to refocus your thoughts and ideas to another topic, or perhaps to slightly shift the way you perceive the idea.

How to Move in Concert with the Flow

Remember to have fun with your thoughts. Even the statement, *the devil is in the detail* (which it is), should be considered with mirth. Know when you place a weighty demand to do something exactly this or that way, you have limited its creation. Do not define everything so precisely. Allow for the sheer merriment of the moment to come forth in a joyous way. Do not limit or constrict how life is able to express itself to or through you or to regulate it in some way.

Enjoy each moment and allow for a little folly to exist in the mix of things. Shift the way you receive and perceive thoughts and ideas. Maybe make a game with whomever you share this teaching. Have fun with these words. When you stay in the flow of consciousness and remain centered in this whirlwind of sorts, you can move mountains of resistance and be in the space you seek so much faster than you thought humanly possible. You might test this out and see how much fun and amazingly effective this premise can be.

Chapter 4

No Opposition, Only Opportunity

The flow of consciousness is how you enable much within your life to unfold with ease and in a most effortless manner. When you surrender, you allow Universe to bring to you what awaits manifestation. It is in the state of *not* knowing, as we have said earlier, that new opportunities are released into your world. You will find new opportunities through the surrender component. Why is this so?

You may be content to express your life as your parents have dictated or perhaps as you believe life has demanded. These may not be those things you have been waiting to bring forward or give birth to, in a manner of speaking. In this way, you can get off-track from what you were destined to do or be. Sometimes life can take you on a ride. If, however, you seek another destiny, then something will present itself to shift you ever closer to the path that calls to you. The shifts will keep occurring until you arrive nearer to what you have wanted to out-picture in this lifetime. Might you reflect now upon what that might be?

No Opposition, Only Opportunity

What awaits is what you have already manifested, and it waits in the expectancy of its birth into this world of form. Let's discuss this. Your co-creations are all those things you create through your thoughts and associated choices. They may have nothing to do with your life work but are what you have brought forward through your thoughts and interpretations — your perceptions via the rose-colored glasses worn during life experiences you've had as this personality — in this lifetime. Although no experience is a mistake, steps can be made that take you away from the path you have chosen. But each step is valuable in that they will show you how certain steps are not preferred, redirecting you in some form or fashion.

What awaits is what you have already manifested ... alludes to something that was envisioned by you prior to embodying here. You also have previously created energetic gifts, termed tools within these writings, that are available and accessible from within your own personal warehouse — your own gift gallery, of sorts. But, too, you can also call upon what is universally accessible. And also, consider a vibration or frequency that allows access to other energetic treasures. These are accessible and attainable when there is a vibrational or energetic match to do so while physically placed.

Do you see when you are in a space of happiness and moving in Universal flow, you operate at a different vibrational

No Opposition, Only Opportunity

frequency than when moving outside of it? When aligned vibrationally, all is accessible and available because you have tuned in to what is already yours to claim but remains slightly out of reach. Once you vibrationally synchronize or align to its frequency, then it can become accessible. This is the true measure of attunement and successfully reaching the measure that will bring you all you seek in this life in a most effortless way. You see, each thing has always been within reach. Access is available through your desire, intention, and focus.

*Tune in now as you
embrace to fully recognize
all is energy, vibration, frequency*

Your purpose is waiting in a full state of readiness and expectancy. Your anticipation of its arrival brings it into being when it becomes physical in your expectancy of it, through your thoughts and feelings. You feel it when you align with it vibrationally. It is there awaiting your alignment in a state of pure potentiality. Your thoughts and vibration align with it when you are in this state of true manifestation.

Now from this state of conscious creation, vision, and expectation, you can begin anew. Let us explain what we mean here. It is from a state of anticipation and expectancy that a vibrational component enters into the equation. There is a degree or frequency that is created during the creation process. So it is not the actual

No Opposition, Only Opportunity

product being conceived but the vibration or the feeling component you sought to experience. It is attaching to and resonating with this vibrational component, which allows for the manifestation to be brought vibrationally into the physical realm.

It is from this state of expectation to allow what is to be. Not mentally knowing, but allowing from a state of surrender so that all might flow and fall into its aligned space. Perform your day with the belief that all you seek is already here, as you behold it inwardly, in its fully manifested form. No opposition — only opportunity exists here.

It is a miraculous and marvelous thing when all falls into place, and this does occur. You see, all must be aligned for this to happen. All of heaven lights up to the glory of this, for it is truly an amazing sight to behold … when all components fall into place for such a manifestation to be made physical.

Chapter 5

We Seek and Find

As we move from this to that, from unconscious creation to consciously creating, let us pause for this understanding to become internalized into the inner core of your being.

It is often heard, but not fully understood, how this can be. So many lifestreams do not yet outwardly know what their purpose is and how to go about determining what it is.

The Little Book to Find Your Purpose

They seek to find it and begin in the doings of it before too much more time passes.

This is also referred to as your reason for being. How do you align to recognize and know what it is? Have you stayed centered now that you know how to get into the flow of consciousness — how to enter into the whirlwind of this synergistic flow, and how to stay there? Then, how to learn or seek to find that which has seemingly eluded you until now? What is it that makes your heart sing with joy and happiness as you enter into doing a task that leads you to the next one? In doing them, does joy spring up as these activities so resonate with you that you glow with happiness? Have you tried for a time to be — to simply be as you see what thoughts enter in?

We Seek and Find

Do you agree that sometimes you just have to slow down a bit and still your mind in order to see what is waiting around the next corner? Sometimes, busywork gets in the way. You must, from time to time, determine what is meaningful to do. And decide what is simply busywork that consumes your time without having much merit. For you do not see (in this moment) what is just beyond your grasp. All the doings or actions are not how you connect to that Part of you, which is aware of what you do not see right now. For you see, you cannot connect to that Part of you which has less connection with the doings but is all-expansive when you are Being.

Do you hear the small voice that offers insights and guidance? That is not ego …

it is surely something else. Observe this as you look within for a more deeply held understanding as you engage internal counsel. Did your parents or those who gave you early direction in life tell you to seek such inner awareness? So many answers do lie within.

Seek to still the mind by utilizing the verses provided earlier. Consider doing so again once all of its components are more fully understood. This process is yet another tool to add to your toolkit of awareness. Seek to access, employ, and mentally disengage in this way — routinely.

When you still the mind and look within, insights will most certainly appear. Don't look elsewhere, for you already have all the necessary components. As Dorothy found in *The Wizard of Oz*, she already had all she needed to get her to where she longed to be. She discovered she'd had this ability throughout her travels but didn't know it until she had taken many detours and laid claim to numerous adventures. In the end, Dorothy discovered she'd already possessed all she needed to return home.

Know that you would never have been left here stranded, so to speak, without all the necessary tools to allow for a successful, almost miraculous outcome. Manifest all you desire in this life. Many have become so distracted with trivial pursuits, such as looking youthful, materialism, and social media activities, in who is doing what — that no one is minding the storehouse of their own treasures. If you are always looking elsewhere, who is present to handle things on your homefront? Know that while this sort of connectedness is a remarkable thing, most things in excess tend to be a bit too much. When overindulgence is preferred, tarry in the arms of the Loving embrace Universal Love offers. It will indulge you in unbounded ways and is an excess that will *not* overwhelm or unbalance you. Satiate in this and perhaps *not* that.

Chapter 6

Love — the Underlying Key to It All

Might you consider now Universal Love as we contemplate its *Loving embrace*? Do you see how one thing does lead to the other? And so when you return to the earlier verses given, invoke and engage this Love. Let us tarry as we begin in a way of Loving measure as we move into Love's expansive and boundless portal that will always and unceasingly embrace, nurture, heal and restore.

So do recognize you have a Loving Aspect that wants your every success. Universe, God, Father, Mother are all terms for the Higher Source that seeks to offer direction and guidance. We recognize the term love is underutilized and not always connected to the unlimited potential of Universal Love. Engage now with its fuller measure to energetically evoke a vibrational frequency, unlike any other. Engage with this frequency in a more conscious way.

Love is indeed an emotion. But it is so much more than what most routinely associate with it. When its full efficacy is discovered upon the broader interpretation, it is consciously internalized and put into

Love — the Underlying Key to It All

play. With this understanding, Love can become more expansive when you release its vast energy as you engage with it in this way. Call it into action within your world and into this physical octave with intention and purpose as you squarely place your focus upon utilizing it in its fuller measure and limitless potential.

What do we mean by this? Love has an energetic vibration that elevates and raises the vibratory frequency when it is consciously called into being. This activates its unique and expansive healing potential. When tapping into love this way, at this level, when you invoke this Love, it evokes an accelerated frequency.

So when you align with Love and the aspect of Love as you focus upon it now, rather than engaging its more common definition, you can enter into Love's all-encompassing vibration as your energy is buoyed into another vibrational frequency. If you have not felt this in the past, you might pause to feel this energy as you consciously invoke it now.

Your energy reacts to match its vibration, as will anything which comes into contact with it. As it moves out into the world of form, it will elevate the vibration of everything in its path before returning back to you.

Seek to no longer limit Love or simply equate it to a physical emotion — an emotion that defines a certain way to feel toward another person or thing. Recognize and now feel how Father and

Love — the Underlying Key to It All

Mother Earth feel toward all of Earth's inhabitants, how the Angelic Kingdom feel toward humankind, how Beings of Light, Universe, God feel toward all creatures from all Kingdoms. By taking this one intentional step, a frequency is created that resonates differently. Tap into this frequency by consciously feeling their Love and focused devotion. Do so by coordinating your mind's eye with your heart center. Through this combined action, in time, you will feel the full efficacy and expansiveness of this Love.

It is from this perspective that you might now express this word and draw all of its kind back to you as it then moves out into the world. It is through the full circle approach of bringing back, complete unto you, what you have put forth as it increases accordingly. When you feel the effect of what you have introduced vibrationally, you will understand its limitless expanse.

This vibrational aspect has been readily accessible yet not often consciously employed in recent times. Now with this one added understanding, more is offered, and its true potential can be realized. Consciously utilize, engage, and invoke this concept of Love. See the results of this energy when purposefully introduced once again into the physical realm.

Expansive opportunities await as you recognize the ability to engage all of life and Universe from a different vantage. From this stance, you can move mountains within your world and thus reap any

Love — the Underlying Key to It All

desired outcome more quickly than before.

All of life wants your success; wants you to have all you seek. Wants you to find what has remained hidden for a time, and with your continued focus, conscious Love, and devotion … can you now see how all is truly possible?

Even the spin of an atom can be recalibrated when engaged to utilize a different vibrational frequency.

All is energy, vibration, frequency.

And so it is.

About the Elders

Think upon Us as a Consciousness of Light and Love. Think upon Us as ever-moving light that does fluctuate and form words within the in-breath and out-breath of a beat or measure. Think upon Us as Love, in Love with all that is. We are Beings that wish for humanity to have answers that have eluded them in recent times. There are those who have shared such information, but it is also being released in this manner, in this time, so there might be a profound knowingness as one engages with life here. We are Pure Consciousness. We are many, and We provide insights for humanity so that more might be gleaned in this lifetime than without such knowledge. We are Love, but all are that which is.

About the Author

Robyn G. Locke bridges the physical with the nonphysical world to bring you purpose-driven, self-healing, self-help books. She is a transformation facilitator, gifted speaker, energy intuitive, and spiritual seeker. *Love life and even what appears to be bad. Discover the deeper meaning attached to each thing encountered along the way. Engage in life's mystery.*

Her inspirational writings are given by the Elders. They provide invaluable insights and suggest refreshingly simple steps to engage. Imagine your future when mental constructs are removed and replaced with purposeful direction. Unbounded opportunities await as you consciously co-create all you desire to manifest.

Discover more at
www.AdvancedEnergetics.org

Find Our Books

BOOK TWO
The Original Purpose
ANSWERS THE AGE-OLD QUESTION — *Why Am I Here?*

Perhaps you've heard about it, but you haven't quite connected to what your purpose is. Maybe you're already enacting your life purpose but what about this original one? So if you've found your mission in this life, do you feel complete, fulfilled, or whole? Might you find your answers when you locate the original one? Discover your original purpose, find the gift in each adversity, and enlist change as you:

- Answer the age-old question, Why am I here?
- Reclaim your life, gain self-awareness, to become self-fulfilled
- Discover why asking questions, and more questions in the in-between time, is vital and key
- Connect to what you are meant to remember during your journey here
- Seek to get about implementing your purpose in a more expansive way
- Embrace change and some foundational truths as your trusted friend
- Employ steps to end the endless mental chatter
- Take steps to recognize and enact your original purpose as you seek to discover more

Step into a greater awareness as you move away from the proclivities of a mental knowingness that brought you adjacent to where you sought to be. Allow new insights to guide you back on course. Access what has been about you and within arms reach all along. Find those things that were always accessible yet had remained unknown.

BOOK THREE
Enact Your Purpose
THEN REACH FOR THE STARS

Discover a powerful means of transformation through compelling and thought-provoking guidance.

Tired of the mind games? Is it time to outwit the wit? Are you intrigued by what could lie outside the physicality of what you can more readily see and touch?

Enact Your Purpose was intuitively given to assist seekers to become more consciously aware and connected to what has been lost over time. With each understanding given, you'll draw new measures into action, redirect mental distractions, and unearth the deeper meaning of emotions. In this intriguing exploration of purposeful discovery, Locke bridges the physical with the nonphysical world and relates loving teachings that will gently guide you to pursue profound insights and change the way you see your life and this world.

In *Enact Your Purpose*, you'll discover:
- The steps to see past the endless mental banter as you understand why you are not your thoughts
- Energetic keys to elevate your frequency and help you to unlock the underlying premise of your purpose
- Effective ways to enact change as you implement some simple steps that will transform your existence, revolutionize how you see this life, and much, much more!

Enact Your Purpose is an invaluable resource to help you on your road to becoming satisfied and fulfilled. If you like thought-provoking guidance, mind-expanding knowledge easily implemented through simple instruction, and the means for transformative change, then you'll love Robyn G. Locke and the Elders' potent shift in perception.

Awaken
The Definitive Guide for Transformative Change

Do you have trouble manifesting what you want in life? Discover how to align your being and tap into those unlimited possibilities.

Feel like you're off-course? Hurdles stopping you in your tracks? Searching for guidance that seems no where to be found? Gifted speaker, change facilitator, and energy intuitive Robyn G. Locke conveys wisdoms given by the Elders – Beings of Pure Consciousness and Infinite Awareness. And now she's here to share powerful Universal insights to spark the means to enact a personal renewal of ultimate self-discovery.

Awaken: The Definitive Guide for Transformative Change is the must-have handbook for seekers desiring to co-create their best life. Its many exercises, relatable stories, meditational offerings, and other insightful approaches will help you release undesired negative energy and overcome those seemingly ever-present obstacles. Utilize new understandings and their platforms of possibility and promise as you relinquish self-limiting beliefs and discover new vistas.

In *Awaken*, you'll discover:

- How to easily, personally, and more readily transform your existence into one that manifests your dreams and desires
- Ways to unlayer and remove trapped emotional energy to help you shift-change into all you might be
- Instruction on the importance of your purpose and how you can step into this new pathway with confidence and ease
- Techniques that will self-heal, create wellness, and lead you to a more lasting happiness
- The ability to access inner fulfillment, shift-change your energy, see this life differently, and so much more

Awaken is an extraordinary resource accelerating the process of true inner awareness, restorative healing, and personal transformation. If you like enacting inspirational insights, garnering a deeper understanding of Universal Love's vast capabilities and timeless teachings, then get ready for the soul-stirring results these new discoveries will bring.

Are you ready to transform into more than your mind can currently fathom?

Awaken Companion Workbook

Utilize the *Companion Workbook* when you need more of a methodology of action and one concise location to further reflect, actuate and move forward all you seek to put into play this day. Enlist and enact those components that will elicit self-healing. Remove the seeds of disease and illness as you manifest a better tomorrow. Bring about change as you foster a healthier body and more than you ever thought possible.

Journal your way to an awakened life.

Connect

Find us at

www.AdvancedEnergetics.org

Facebook: @AdvancedEnergetics

Instagram: @AdvancedEnergetics

Twitter: @theEldersListen

YouTube: AdvancedEnergetics